DOGS

POODLES

STUART A. KALLEN

ABDO & Daughters

Published by Abdo & Daughters, 4940 Viking Drive, Suite 622, Edina, Minnesota 55435.

Library bound edition distributed by Rockbottom Books, Pentagon Tower, P.O. Box 36036, Minneapolis, Minnesota 55435.

Printed in the United States.

Cover Photo credit: Peter Arnold, Inc.

Interior Photo credits: Peter Arnold, Inc.

Edited by Rosemary Wallner

Library of Congress Cataloging-in-Publication Data

Kallen, Stuart A., 1955   Poodle / Stuart A. Kallen.
     p. cm. — (Dogs)
   Includes bibliographical references (p.24) and index.
   ISBN 1-56239-451-7
1. Poodles—Juvenile literature. [1. Poodles. 2. Dogs.] I. Title. II. Series Kallen, Stuart A., 1955- Dogs.
SF429.P85K28   1995
636.7'2—dc20
                                               95-927
                                               CIP
                                               AC

ABOUT THE AUTHOR
Stuart Kallen has written over 80 children's books, including many environmental science books.

Contents

DOGS AND WOLVES: CLOSE COUSINS

Dogs have been living with humans for more than 12,000 years. Today, hundreds of millions of dogs live in the world. Over 400 **breeds** exist.

All dogs are related to the wolf. Some dogs—like tiny poodles or Great Danes—may look nothing like the wolf. But under their skin, every dog shares many feelings and **traits** with the wolf.

All dogs are related to the wolf.

POODLES

When people think of poodles, they imagine dogs with fluffy haircuts tied up with bows. But poodles are one of the oldest dog **breeds** in the world. They have been around for almost 2,000 years.

The first poodles were called "water dogs." The word "poodle" is taken from a German word that means "to swim like a dog." Poodles were used to **retrieve** ducks, geese, and swans during a hunt. To help them swim better, their **coats** were shaved very short. That is why poodles are **sheared**.

Poodles often have fluffy haircuts tied up with bows.

WHAT THEY'RE LIKE

Poodles come in three sizes. Toy poodles are small. Miniature poodles are medium-sized. Standard poodles are the largest.

Toy poodles were first **bred** in Spain. Spanish women carried their poodles everywhere. The poodle kept people's hands warm during cold weather. This earned toy poodles the name "sleeve dogs."

Medium poodles were trained as **retrievers**. Standard poodles were once the most popular poodle. They were trained as hunters and war dogs. They are excellent swimmers and very smart.

The poodle's grace, intelligence, and happy nature have made it one of the most popular dogs in America. Today, poodles are number five on the top ten list of popular dogs.

Poodles come in three sizes. Toy poodles are small. Miniature poodles are medium sized. Standard poodles are the largest.

COAT AND COLOR

All types of poodles have thick, curly, double **coats**. The **undercoat** is short and dense. The top coat is longer.

Some poodles have a soft, curly top coat. It is straight when brushed but turns curly after a few hours. Other poodles have a "steel wool" top coat that forms kinky curls.

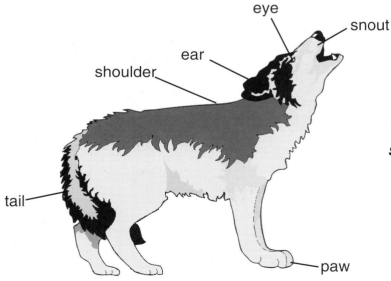

eye

snout

ear

shoulder

tail

paw

All dogs share the same features with their common ancestor, the wolf.

All poodles have thick, curly, double coats.

Purebred poodles never have straight hair. Most poodles are either black or white. But they may also be blue, brown, silver, apricot, beige, or cream.

SIZE

The three types of poodles are different sizes. The adult standard poodle is 22 inches (56 cm) from the ground to its shoulders. A miniature poodle stands 10 to 15 inches (25 to 38 cm) tall. The toy poodle is 10 inches (25 cm) and under.

Standard poodles weigh about 60 pounds (27 kg). Miniatures weigh about 14 to 18 pounds (6 to 8 kg). Toy poodles weigh about 6 to 12 pounds (3 to 5 kg).

A well-**bred** poodle has a noble face with a round head and flat cheekbones. The **muzzle** is long and straight. The almond-shaped eyes are set wide apart.

A well-bred poodle has a noble face with a round head and flat cheekbones.

CARE

Poodles fit in well with most families. They are gentle, loving, playful and carefree. Like all dogs, poodles need the same things that humans need: a warm bed, food, water, exercise, and lots of love.

Poodles need **grooming** every few days. If the dog is not groomed, its beautiful **coat** will become matted and tangled. Sometimes, the dog will need a bath and its nails clipped. Professional groomers can cut the hair on the poodle's face, paws, and tail.

Poodles are gentle, loving, playful and carefree.

FEEDING

Like all dogs, poodles enjoy meat. But poodles need a well-balanced diet. Most dog foods—dry or canned—will give the dog proper **nutrition**.

When you buy a puppy, find out what it has been eating and continue that diet. A small puppy needs four to five small meals a day. By six months, it will need only two meals a day. By one year, a single evening feeding will be enough.

Like any animal, poodles need a lot of fresh water. Keep a full dish of water next to the dog's food bowl and change it daily.

Poodles need a well-balanced diet.

THINGS THEY NEED

Dogs need a quiet place to sleep. A soft dog bed in a quiet corner is the best place for a poodle to sleep.

Poodles should live indoors. If the dog must live outside, give it a dry, **insulated** dog house.

In most cities and towns, dogs must be leashed when going for a walk.

Dogs also need a license. Dog licenses have the owner's name, address, and telephone number on them. If the dog runs away, the owners can be called.

All dogs need a license which they wear around their neck.

PUPPIES

Average poodles can have three to five puppies each time they give birth. The dog is **pregnant** for about nine weeks. When she is ready to give birth, she needs a dark place away from noises. If your dog is pregnant, give her a strong box lined with an old blanket. She will have her puppies there.

Puppies are tiny and helpless when born. They arrive about half an hour apart. The mother licks them clean which helps them start breathing. Their eyes are shut, making them blind for their first nine days. They are also deaf for about ten days.

Dogs are **mammals**. They drink milk from their mother. After about four weeks, puppies will grow teeth. Separate them from their mother and give the puppies soft dog food.

A poodle with her puppies.

GLOSSARY

BREED - A grouping of animals with the same traits; also, to produce young.

COAT - The dog's outer covering (hair).

GROOM - To brush and take care of an animal.

INSULATION (in-sue-LAY-shun) - Something that stops heat loss.

MAMMAL - A class of animals, including humans, that have hair and feed their young milk.

MUZZLE - The jaws, mouth, and nose of an animal.

NUTRITION (new-TRISH-un) - Food; nourishment.

PREGNANT - With one or more babies growing inside the body.

PUREBRED - Bred from members of one breed within a species.

RETRIEVE - To return or bring back.

SHEARING - To cut the dogs hair.

TRAIT - A characteristic or feature of the animal.

UNDERCOAT - An animal's coat that is under the top coat and closest to the skin.

Index

BIBLIOGRAPHY

American Kennel Club. *The Complete Dog Book.* New York: Macmillan, 1992.

Clutton-Brock, Juliet. *Dog.* New York: Alfred A. Knopf, 1991.

The Complete Book of the Dog. New York: Holt, Rinehart, & Winston, 1985.

Sylvester, Patricia. *The Reader's Digest Illustrated Book of Dogs.* New York: The Reader's Digest Association, 1984.